# *DRAGON KNIGHT*

by Adam Bushnell and Leo Trinidad

FRANKLIN WATTS
LONDON·SYDNEY

# DRAGON KNIGHT

## CONTENTS

| | | |
|---|---|---|
| Chapter 1 | Dragon Attack! | 4 |
| Chapter 2 | George and the Dragon | 7 |
| Chapter 3 | Curfew in London | 10 |
| Chapter 4 | To the Tower | 14 |
| Chapter 5 | Into the Dragon's Lair | 19 |
| Chapter 6 | The Music of Dragons | 22 |

# CHAPTER 1

# DRAGON ATTACK!

"Ladies and gentlemen, this is an emergency broadcast." Nick and his mum stopped what they doing and looked at the television screen. The newsreader's voice sounded urgent. Something serious must have happened.

"Some time ago, we received reports of a creature flying over London. At first it was thought to be a kind of dinosaur but experts have confirmed that the creature is actually a dragon." The screen was now showing mobile phone footage of what looked exactly like a dragon flapping across a grey sky. Nick looked up at his mum. This had to be a joke, right? A dragon? The newsreader continued:

"Emergency services have been called to the scene. People have been told to stay inside their houses until further notice."

Nick's eyes widened. So it was true – this was actually happening. The police wouldn't be involved if it was a prank. But a dragon? Here in England? Dragons weren't real. They were creatures of myth and legend from long ago, weren't they?

The newsreader went on but Nick barely heard her. He was lost in his own thoughts. He looked back at the footage of the dragon, now in close-up. The dragon was an emerald green colour and covered in large scales with vast sail-like wings that helped the massive creature slice effortlessly through the sky. Two curved horns skimmed the clouds and yellow slitted eyes scanned the land below as if searching for food. Its mouth was full of razor-sharp teeth.

Then it dipped and raced towards the earth. The film blurred for a moment as the camera struggled to keep up with the dragon's speed. When the picture came back into focus, the dragon was hovering above a house. Suddenly it zoomed downwards and landed with a heavy thud in a garden. It lunged towards a large pond. It chomped and guzzled. It was feeding on the fish! Then it spread its vast wings and took off again.

Nick sat and stared at the television in disbelief. He and his mum stayed there, standing in the kitchen, as reports of dragon sightings continued throughout the day.

Nick noticed that the dragon wasn't actually attacking people. Each time it landed, it fed on fish from ponds, lakes, rivers and streams.

This gave Nick an idea. He raced to his room.

## CHAPTER 2

## GEORGE AND THE DRAGON

Nick looked around and found the book he had brought home from school just last night. The title was *George and the Dragon*. It was about a knight from England who had killed a dragon. Perhaps it would have some suggestions for how people could protect themselves. He scanned the pages. The dragon in this book terrorised the land, spitting out fire and burning down everything in its path. The king ordered knights to kill the dragon but none of them succeeded. So the king tried something different. He ordered everyone to feed the dragon. But then the food ran out. The king became desperate and ordered that everyone should draw straws to decide who would be fed to the dragon.

Straw was distributed to all the people across the land. Whoever picked the shortest straw would be fed to the dragon. But it just so happened that the king's own daughter got the short straw. Even though the king was devastated, the same rules had to be applied. The princess was tied to a large post and left for the dragon to eat. But when the dragon turned up, so did Saint George, a heroic knight, who slayed the dragon and saved the princess.

"This is all a bit unbelievable," Nick said aloud to his empty room, "but it seems it is happening again. A dragon has found its way here. Who will save us this time?"

Then Nick noticed an information section in the back of the book, after the story. It explained how the flag of England was named the St George's Cross to honour the knight who had saved the country from the dragon.

Nick placed the book on his bed and went back down to the kitchen. His mum was still standing there, staring at the television. The dragon was soaring across the sky on the hunt for more food. But, unlike in the book Nick had just read, this dragon wasn't actually hurting anyone. Perhaps this dragon might just be lost and confused. Perhaps it might need someone's help.

# CHAPTER 3

## CURFEW IN LONDON

Dragon sightings were still on television three days later. The news footage showed it flying across London during the day. Then, as night fell, it followed the River Thames over London Bridge towards the Tower of London.

Nick wondered if it had made some sort of home in the Tower. Perhaps it slept in the grounds.

Nick knew the Tower of London well. His Uncle Reggie was a guide there and Nick had often gone on tours with him. There would be no tours for a while, though. The Prime Minister had ordered a curfew and everyone had to stay inside. No one could leave their homes. There were no shops open, no cars on the road, no work for Mum and no school. Nick was rather pleased about that, but really the whole thing did seem a bit ridiculous. As far as anyone could tell, the dragon hadn't actually done anything. Sure, it looked scary. Sure, it ate a lot of fish. But no one had been hurt. Nothing had been damaged. Perhaps this particular dragon was not like the one he had read about in the story.

Nick sighed as he looked out of his window. The flat where he and his mum lived was above a row of shops. He loved the view they had. He could see the River Thames and even the Tower if he craned his neck far enough.

Nick hadn't been to school for three days now and he was getting bored. Mum wasn't much company, either. She was busy on the phone calling all their relatives, even those in Jamaica, reassuring them that she and Nick weren't in danger. Nick sighed again. The darkening sky seemed to match his mood. Then he gasped as he saw the dragon come racing across the horizon. Nick opened the balcony door and slipped outside. He had seen the dragon a few times now and it fascinated him. He peered and strained his eyes to see it dip down towards the Tower.

The television reporters had discussed and debated where it might be hiding. The armed forces had been using high-tech equipment to try and track it down but no one had managed to trace where it spent its time sleeping.

Nick was pretty sure that it must be hiding in the Tower – it was the obvious place. Having been on Uncle Reggie's tours so many times, Nick knew the Tower like the back of his hand, and he knew there were secret tunnels and caves underneath it. The rocks were too thick to be scanned by radar technology.

He slipped back inside the flat. Perhaps he could find the dragon? His mother wouldn't want him to, of course, but he could sneak out when she was asleep and be back before she could worry.

Nick looked at the television. There was yet another report discussing why this so-called scary dragon had to be destroyed. But Nick knew it wasn't evil. Somehow, he just knew it. He would show everyone that sometimes stories in books are just that; stories. The dragon wasn't bad. Nick just had to prove it.

## CHAPTER 4

## TO THE TOWER

That night, when Mum came in to kiss Nick goodnight, he was already tucked up in bed. He waited until he was sure Mum was asleep then he leapt up from under the covers, fully dressed. Grabbing his torch, he crept out like a cat burglar into the gloomy London night. The streets were deserted. Normally, he wouldn't have dreamt of going out at night on his own but these were extraordinary circumstances. There were no people, no cars, no buses; London was a ghost town.

Nick arrived at the Tower and began scanning the walls to find a way underneath.

After a while, near to where the Tower Zoo once was, Nick spotted a small door that led to a descending passageway. This part of the Tower was unfamiliar to him – he hadn't been down there on Uncle Reggie's tours. Reggie had told Nick that it led to dangerous caves and tunnels. Nick swallowed hard, then steadied himself.

He pulled out the small torch he had slipped into his pocket and turned it on. This made little difference but offered some comfort at least. He walked on for what seemed like hours, following the dim light of his torch. Then, in the distance, he saw a figure. But it was not the dragon; the passageway was too narrow for that. It looked like a human.

"Er, hello?" he called out uncertainly into the darkness.

"Greetings," a voice called back.

It was a man. Nick sighed with relief. This must be someone who worked at the Tower. He was probably hiding from the dragon down here.

Nick shone the torch over the figure that stood in front of him and gasped. The man wore armour like a knight, but it wasn't shining armour like the knights wore in the books Nick had read. This knight's armour was filthy, and covered in dents and scratches.

Surely this couldn't be a real knight. Perhaps he was one of those people called re-enactors. Nick had seen these at the Tower before. Re-enactors dressed as people from the past to entertain the visitors. That's it – surely this knight was a re-enactor.

Nick shone the torch toward the man's face. He had thick, tousled brown hair and an unruly brown beard. The dark eyes showed kindness behind them.

Nick approached the knight and held out his hand.

"Hi, I'm Nick," he said.

"And I am George."

A gauntleted hand gripped Nick's arm as a greeting.

"Are you one of those guys off the telly who pretend to be knights?" Nick asked.

George looked puzzled. "What is a telly, my friend?"

Nick shook his head in disbelief. "Telly – TV – Television? It doesn't matter," he said, bewildered. "What are you doing down here?"

"I seek the dragon," George replied. "He has escaped my world and found his way here. I am bound to find him and restore him to his rightful time and place."

"Your world?" Nick asked hesitatingly.

"This is not my world," came the mysterious reply. "Is it yours? Why are you here, Nick?"

"I came to find the dragon, too. I don't think it's bad like everyone says it is. I just want to help."

George smiled broadly. "Then I have a companion on my journey!" he cried, clapping Nick on the shoulder with his gauntleted hand. "Come! We will track it together!"

## CHAPTER 5

## INTO THE DRAGON'S LAIR

Nick stared at the knight. His armour and weapons certainly looked very real. He spoke in a strange way. He sounded like someone from the old adventure movies his gran watched. A shield was strapped to his back. It had a red cross on a white background like the England flag.

"Oh! You're Saint George, aren't you?" Nick said.

"Who?" George asked.

"You're a great knight!" Nick exclaimed, "England's patron saint! I've just read a book about you."

"Me? A saint?" George roared with laughter.

"But you are him, aren't you?" Nick insisted. "You killed a dragon. You saved England. Our flag is named after you."

"Nick, my friend, I am from the Eastern lands, not England. And I do not kill dragons. I tame them and help them to live in peace with people. I have travelled all over the world doing this. I have seen many dragons. Ones with wings, others without. Ones that breathe fire, others ice or steam. Some with antlers, others with horns. Dragons are rare and beautiful creatures, not something to kill. But sadly, some people will kill what they do not understand."

"I thought you were an English knight who killed a dragon and married a princess," said Nick.

George laughed again. "This is my first time in England and I have met no princesses. Only you, my friend!"

He grabbed Nick by the shoulders. "Come, let us track the dragon together and help him back to my world. Leave the rest to me. I can return this beautiful creature to where it will be more at home. Quietly now, so as not to disturb our friend."

Nick and George made an unlikely pair as they set off through the gloom, led only by the light of Nick's small torch. George's armour clinked and rattled as they went, making their journey anything but quiet.

At last, the narrow passageway gave way to a vast underground cave. A shaft of light beamed down from a gap in the top. It illuminated a gigantic snoring shape on the cave floor. Emerald scales glistened in the moonlight.

"We are here," George whispered. "Prepare yourself."

Climbing carefully over jagged rocks, the pair moved slowly towards the sleeping dragon. Its deep snores filled the space entirely.

Nick looked at the knight at his side. Saint George, the tamer of dragons was with him – not the slayer of dragons he had read about in a book. Somehow, someone who tamed dragons was more encouraging.

# CHAPTER 6

# THE MUSIC OF DRAGONS

The knight pointed at the dragon and then back at Nick. He was miming something. But it wasn't what Nick was expecting. George appeared to be asking Nick to wake the dragon up!

Nick shook his head. He wasn't going to be that stupid – he would be eaten or squashed or something! But George was smiling. He took off the shield that was strapped to his back, flipped it over and pulled free an ancient harp from some leather straps.

George continued nodding and pointing furiously for Nick to hurry. Nick gulped and stepped forward. The knight nodded again but slowly and more encouragingly now.

Nick took a deep breath and walked towards the sleeping dragon. He whispered very quietly, "Hello?"

Nothing. The dragon snored on.

"Hello?" Nick called, a little louder this time.

Still nothing.

**"Hello!"**

And three things happened simultaneously; the dragon's eyes snapped open, it pushed itself up on to its claws and opened its mouth, revealing its sharp teeth. Nick closed his eyes and prepared himself for the end.

But the end did not come. Nick opened first one eye and then the other. He was still alive. An enchanting sound had filled the cave. It was the most beautiful music that Nick had ever heard.

George was standing at the other side of the cave playing the ancient harp and singing softly in a language Nick could not understand. It was such a beautiful piece of music that, despite the situation he found himself in, Nick smiled.

The dragon moved slowly towards the knight. It seemed hypnotised by the sound.

George walked towards the tail. The dragon's head followed the sound of the singing and the harp. George then walked in large circles and the dragon followed him. Its head and tail were now touching, making a perfect circle.

George stepped on to the tail and walked along the back between vicious-looking spikes.

George sat on the dragon's head. He had stopped singing but continued to play the harp.

"This is the Harp of Orpheus," George said, smiling.

"I got it from my grandfather. He discovered it when he fought for the Roman army in Greece. He was a dragon tamer, too."

"How will you get back to your world?" asked Nick.

"The same way I . . . we . . . got here," George replied, taking out a gnarled and twisted stick from his armour.

Nick's eyes were as wide as when he had first seen the dragon on the television in his kitchen.

George was holding what must be a wand and was uttering strange, magical words.

The air around the knight and dragon fizzed with electricity, the dragon's green scales reflecting light around the cave.

"Farewell, Nick!" called George. "We will leave you now. Thank you for your company!"

Both he and the dragon were fading as they flew away, their bodies quickly disappearing into the light that enveloped them.

"Thank you, George," Nick cried out. "Goodbye and good luck!"

And they were gone. The light faded to nothing and Nick was left alone in the darkness of the cave. He stood silently for a while, recent events whirling through his mind.

Then he took his little torch out of his pocket, turned it on and walked slowly back the way he had come.

He had met a real dragon, and he had met England's greatest knight. They hadn't been characters from a book, they had been real.

Eventually, Nick emerged into fresh air. It seemed even darker now as he moved quickly and quietly back to his flat through the still deserted streets.

He slipped back into the flat and listened. He could hear soft snoring from his mum's room. Everything was as it was. He had done it. Well, George had done it. The dragon was back where it belonged and life could return to normal in England.

Nick changed into his pyjamas and slipped into bed. He switched on the torch again and grabbed his book from the bedside table. Turning to the picture of the Saint George's Cross, he noticed a section under the picture of the flag that he hadn't read earlier. It said that the red cross represented strength and the white background represented peace. Strength and peace. George would be happy with that. Especially the peace part. Nick smiled and fell fast asleep.

## Things to think about

1. Do you like the modern-day setting for the legendary characters of St George and the dragon? Why / why not?
2. What impression do you get of Nick's character at the start of the story? Does this change as the story develops?
3. Did you already know the story of St George and the Dragon? If we had large, fire-breathing dragons around today, how do you think they might live alongside humans?
4. What do you know about the Tower of London? Is this a good home for the dragon in your opinion?
5. What do you think about the character of St George in this story?

## Write it yourself

Some of the themes in this story are thinking independently, self-belief, magic, respect and friendship. Choose one, or more, of these themes and try to write your own story.
Plan your story before you begin to write it.
Start off with a story map:
- a beginning to introduce the characters and where and when your story is set (the setting);
- a problem which the main characters will need to fix in the story;
- an ending where the problems are resolved.

Get writing! Try to include physical reaction to show what your characters are feeling, for example:
Nick swallowed hard.